Introduction

The Blame Stops Here

Honesty. It's such a lonely word. We've all heard that before thanks to Billy Joel. But it's not just lonely. It's also mostly one-sided when it comes to our thoughts about honesty. We often think about it as it relates to how we act and what we say to others. But what about being honest with ourselves? I'm not talking about thinking that you look good in a leisure suit or sandals with socks. I'm talking about being completely honest and objective about our perception on everything around us. As you read through this book keep that question in mind.

All too often we have been pulled away from being honest with ourselves and drawn into a game of blaming others for bad situations. Just how crazy has our society become with playing "the blame game?" It's everywhere from media to politics to our very own casual conversations. We have become so conditioned to it that we don't even notice it unless it's pointed out to us. What is "the blame game" you ask? Well, simply put, it's not accepting responsibility and blaming others for outcomes that you don't care for in your life. Those "others" could be people, corporations, governments or circumstances. Sure there are any numbers of famous (and profitable) examples of blame involving liability litigation such as the hot coffee spill incident at McDonald's. But as humorous and maddening as they may be, they have an effect on our own lives and how we take responsibility for our actions (or lack of).

Do you make yourself a victim and play "the blame game" in your own life? Think about it. Have you

blamed being overweight on genetics?

blamed your child's or your own poor grades on a teacher?

blamed your lack of job satisfaction on your boss, co-workers or the company?

blamed the other person for a failed relationship?

blamed others for the person you are today?

If you have then you're like most people in that you've pointed the finger of responsibility away from yourself many times. Do not fret my friend. Today is your Independence Day. Think about how wonderful it would be if you could have the chance to rid yourself of all of those "blame" issues. Think about how awesome it would be to find somebody who could help you to change your life for the better and stop being victimized. You're in luck. Read on and feel the liberation and empowerment of being personally responsible. Experience the true satisfaction to achieve on your own terms. The best part about it is that you have all of the tools that you need, namely YOU.

Once you accept the fact that you are responsible for your situation (and that you don't look good wearing sandals with socks), you quickly realize that you are also the solution. Sit back and enjoy a somewhat serious look at life and how you can break free and escape from the prison of blame and go from being a victim to victory.

Table Of Contents

1

A Funny Thing Happened on the Way to Liability

Help! Save Me!

There's an old joke that members of the clergy have told to their congregations for years. It goes something like this. A heavy rainstorm was closing in on a small town. All of the townspeople were told to evacuate because of imminent flooding. The local priest, who wanted to remain inside his church to ride out the storm, refused to evacuate. A few hours after the torrential rain had begun; water crept up to the steps of the church. Police came by in a rescue boat and told the priest to get in the boat before it's too late. The priest responded, "The Lord will save me. I will remain here with my church." Hours later, the water kept rising and made it all the way up to the windows of the church. Again, police came by in a rescue boat and ordered the priest to leave. Again, he refused and said, "The Lord will save me. I will remain here with my church." Soon after, the water had risen to the roof of the church. This time, the police sent a helicopter and pleaded with the priest, now hanging onto the steeple, to grab hold of the ladder and climb aboard. Again, he refused and said "The Lord will save me..." Sure enough, the water kept rising and the priest met his fate. Upon arriving in heaven, the priest asked God, "Father, why did you abandon me in my time of need?" God answered, "I sent you two boats and a helicopter. What more did you want?"

I'm often reminded of this joke as I see and hear instances of the deterioration of personal responsibility in our society. Typically, we receive plenty of notice and opportunities to make good decisions (or at least the option that improves our situation), just as the priest did. However, all too often we ignore these opportunities and choose an alternative that has a negative effect on our lives. While making poor decisions is something that we all have done and will continue to do, we have unknowingly been trained to take the next step. The training comes from many different areas of our lives including education, media, the court system, politicians, sports and our very own conversations. What is the next step? Well, it's never good enough to simply accept the fact that you have done something that was ill-advised or just downright brainless. No. You need someone or something to blame. You need a scapegoat. You need someone who is responsible for this mess you've gotten yourself into. Someone who is "liable." Yes, "liable." It is perhaps the single most impactful word in our language over the last 40 years. Getting through a week without hearing or seeing the word "liable" or "liability" is virtually impossible. Someone or something always has to be liable and, of course, it's not you. That very powerful word has singlehandedly taken down playgrounds in communities, prevented doctors from performing potential life-saving procedures and created an army of ambulance-chasing attorneys that rivals the Spanish Armada. "Liability" has also created a population of victims. You see, if somebody else is liable for my predicament then I must be the victim. Just think if the priest in our joke played the blame game and steered his situation in the liability direction. He could very easily have blamed the government for not providing him official written warnings, or his cable television provider for not giving him free access to The Weather Channel or God himself for not giving him the natural born ability to swim. The frightening part is that all of those scenarios would be acceptable excuses by many today. In fact, there are plenty of attorneys who would line up to see if a lawsuit was appropriate.

Would You Like Fries With That?

Just how far out of control has the blame-game gotten? It's easy to see because it's everywhere you look. If you're a victim of being overweight you have a number of companies to blame. You've got McDonald's, Burger King and Wendy's for starters. Those evil fat farms broke your will and forced you to eat at their institutions 5 times a week and never once warned you that consuming three fully-loaded cheeseburgers with French fries might lead to a possible increase in waist size. Oh, while you're at it you also have Coke and Pepsi to blame. They didn't give you fair warning that downing a 2-liter bottle of cola every day might not be the best way to trim down. Sounds outrageous, right? Who would even think of something so ridiculous? Well, governments at several levels in the United States are considering that an "obesity tax" be levied against all non-diet soft drinks sold in a town, county, state or even the country. Can fast-food be far behind? As state and federal budgets become extremely obese look for more politicians trying to find ways to make a profit from blaming. Leave it to public officials to provide victory for the victims. But wait, there's more...

Do you have lung cancer or emphysema? Blame the cigarette manufacturers. Is your child not succeeding in school? Blame the school. Blame the teacher. Heck, blame the crossing guard. The prevailing attitude among school parents today places all of the onus of learning on the schools and none of it on themselves. Did you get pregnant or get someone pregnant in high school? You've got a choice here. You can blame the TV and film industry for showing you too much sex. Or you can blame Calvin Klein for too many racy billboards. Your choice. Can't hear that well? Blame Bose or the Apple iPod. Did you lose your job because you weren't performing well? Blame the Chinese. Did you lose your job because of company cost-cutting? Definitely blame China or India, whoever is more convenient for you. Have an erection lasting more than 4 hours? It depends on your situation as to whether you're blaming or thanking someone. If you are going to blame somebody you can always blame the pharmaceutical industry.

In all of these scenarios the common thread is that people choose to ignore or deny the obvious. How many fingers need to be pointed elsewhere before one realizes that he/she is the common denominator? How much weight needs to be put on? How many career opportunities need to be squandered? How many broken relationships never get repaired? When faced with honestly answering these tough questions we often seem to revert back to childhood and employ claims of ignorance such "I didn't know", "I had no idea" or "I didn't know anything was wrong." When we're not truly honest with ourselves these are all knee-jerk reactions that just come out of our mouths from years of conditioning. I suppose it's human nature to take the easier path. Playing the part of the victim is very easy. However, as it has been said many times, there is no free lunch. The convenience of victimhood comes with a steep price. It makes you weak and powerless and shackles you to your current situation, poor decisions and negativity. Essentially you willingly give up your freedom.

Let's Get Down to Business

I hope that what I have written in this book will help you. Not help you in a Tony Robbins sort of way where I pump you up with how you should strive to be a better person and then you run out and do it. No, no, no. What I'm talking about is very practical. It is about recognizing what is going on around you and accepting that you probably got yourself into most of the messes in your life. It is a realization that you, and only you, can get yourself out of them. Let the highly popular blame/excuse bandwagon go right by you and make yourself personally liable for your life. I think you'll find that it's downright liberating, empowering and will make your life exponentially better. This is a "good news" story folks. You have the solution and it's you.

The main motivation for this book is not just helping people to become more personally responsible. It also goes beyond the general public acceptance that blame should be placed elsewhere for bad situations or outcomes. I believe the truly disturbing piece about this topic is the *expectation* that blame must be placed elsewhere. Almost as if it were assumed, you have to blame somebody else for a poor result. Why wouldn't you? It's standard practice, right? If you're not blaming somebody else then there must be something wrong. It's that very attitude that seems to have gained prevalence and is destroying people's lives. We have become so influenced by the "passing of the buck" mentality that consumes news headlines and media. For many it has resulted in a trained response in how they live their lives. For example, if you went to a restaurant and fell down in the parking lot many people would think you are crazy if you did not attempt to sue the restaurant. It's expected. The thought process doesn't end there. It transfers to other situations in life and holding others responsible becomes a habit.

This brings me back to our priest. Had he known how to play the game and not met his demise he could have sued the archdiocese for not preparing him well enough for emergency situations. Was there a course that he was required to take including acknowledgements that he checked off explaining emergency procedures? Better yet, he could have sued any number of publishers (including King James himself) for distributing the Bible's Old Testament which allows us to believe that Moses parted a sea or that Noah survived a 40-day flood in an ark. Think it's far-fetched? Just wait until some mayor or governor of a flood ravaged region proposes a "flood-tax" on any Bible sold in the city or state because of the misleading stories in it. We're not that far away from it. After all, someone needs to fight for the victims.

2

Everyday Occurrences

"Things have been so crazy..."

Why is it so easy for us to blame others for things that don't go well? We could get deeply philosophical and talk about how the ascent of humankind has always been driven by finding easier ways to get things done. From the invention of the wheel to the printing press to the microwave oven humans are always looking for an easier way. Maybe that's why we do resort to blaming so much. It certainly is an easier path. I don't want to get too far into the examination of the evolution of humans. However, we have taken the concept of making things easier and applied it directly our own interpersonal communications. There has been no fanfare over it. No inventor has asked for credit or filed for a patent. Nobody has won any awards as a result of it. It just happened over time. I'll show you what I mean.

Did you ever forget to call somebody back on the telephone? I'm sure you have. As I'm sure you have had people forget to call you back. To make the example more contemporary we should include emailing and texting. Regardless of the delivery method, someone asked you to get back to them and you didn't. Inevitably we have all said at one time or another when finally conversing or writing with that person, "I'm really sorry. Things have been so crazy and I just haven't had any time...blah, blah, blah." We have all done it. We even make it more colorful depending on our personal situations. If you own a business the proper response is "Things have been so crazy down at the shop..." If someone has recently died in your family the proper line is "Things have been so crazy with Ted dying and everything…" If someone is out of work in the family you say "Things have been so crazy with Fred out of work…" Let's take a look at a partial guide:

"Things have been so crazy…

> *since I had my foot amputated after the farming accident…*
> *with my dog getting neutered…*
> *with my daughter finally doing poopies on the potty…*
> *since Frank came out of the closet…*
> *since I combined Activia® with Quaker® Oats and a bowl of prunes…*

that I haven't been able to get back to you"

Even though we have all had these types of conversations some people always manage to up the ante. I can't even count how many times people have used national or international tragedies as excuses for forgetting or ignoring. The list includes tsunamis, terrorist attacks, earthquakes, hurricanes, floods, government overthrows, riots, protests and the Black Plague. "I'm sorry. You know with all of the craziness of the unrest in the Middle East I've just been out of it." People actually associate themselves with real victims of real tragedies to make an excuse. My personal favorite was used in mid-2009 after a string of celebrity deaths including Michael Jackson and Farrah Fawcett. "I just can't believe what's been going on with all these celebrities dying. I've been caught up in the whole thing. I'm sorry I haven't gotten back to you." Really?? Do you honestly believe that I'm going to accept that as an excuse? Then again, why not? All the other ones seem to work.

Why do we feel the need to attach an excuse for forgetting to call someone back? It would be so refreshing if somebody said, "I'm sorry. I completely forgot to call you back." Even the people who experience significant changes in their lives either from death or sickness should say, "I'm sorry. I forgot." Because that is what happened after all. Harsh? Possibly. Truthful? Definitely.

At first glance, the issue of not calling somebody back is relatively minor and certainly not worthy of a crisis alert. After all, just about everybody has done it multiple times. However it is worth noting and is possibly bigger than we think after further review. I believe that this is where lack of personal responsibility and excuse making all starts. Think about it. I'm not responsible for not calling you back. Frank came out of the closet. It's his fault. Rover got neutered and is humping my neighbor's leg every day. It's his fault. Those damn celebrities who died. It's their fault. Al-Qaeda for goodness sake! It's their fault. If I don't need to take responsibility for not returning a phone call then I can apply this to other aspects of my life. Why not? It seems to work well and is perfectly accepted with the phone call. All I do is mention the lame excuse, it's acknowledged by the other party and then we move onto the conversation. I seem to get out of it pretty easily. No harm. No foul. See how easy it is to slide into becoming a victim?

Furthermore, how did you learn to speak on the phone? Where did you learn your phone etiquette? If you're like most people then you learned proper phone technique from your parents. I bet that you answer a phone or ask for somebody on the phone the same way your parents taught you many years ago. Here's something you probably never thought of either. You learned how to make excuses for not calling people back from your parents as well. It's a learned behavior.

The casual acceptance of shirking responsibility has escalated into far more serious issues. Because if you are not responsible then somebody else must be. That means that they are also liable. Ah yes, the magic word. Liable.

"Oh don't be so hard on yourself."

At many points in our lives we have all either consoled someone or have been consoled as the result of something that didn't go well. Because the consoler is trying to make somebody feel better he tries to minimize the role that the person played in the situation. Phrases like "how could you possibly know", "it's not your fault" and of course "oh don't be so hard on yourself" are uttered to raise the spirits of the person who feels down.

I could imagine how this was used throughout history. "Pilate, don't be so hard on yourself. You had no idea he was the Son of God." "General Custer, it's OK. How could you possibly know that thousands of Indians would come out of nowhere like that?" "Prime Minister Chamberlain, don't be so hard on yourself. Who knew Hitler was a bad guy and really wasn't interested in peace?" Maybe these phrases were never said but you never know. Maybe they were.

Humor aside, let's take a look at the more mundane examples we see frequently. A child may inadvertently hurt another child when throwing a ball. The child who threw the ball becomes very upset because he has hurt somebody else. A parent or another adult will try to console the child and say "It's OK. You did nothing wrong. You didn't mean to hurt him." Another example could be an adult who says something in a group setting that causes another adult to think of a tragic time in her life. She becomes visibly upset and leaves the area. The person who made the statement becomes upset as well because he meant no harm. The other adults quickly soften the blow and let him know that it's not his fault and he didn't know that his comments would trigger such a reaction.

In these examples, just like countless other ones in our everyday lives, the consolers are correct. The person who caused the pain shouldn't feel an overwhelming sense of responsibility because there was no intent involved and there is no reasonable evidence to suggest that they should have known better. The point is not to place blame on these individuals and make them accept the responsibility. The point is to shed light on how these common accidents and faux pas moments have been engrained into our thinking and that personal responsibility is immediately lifted in these cases. Just think of a personal situation where a consoler did *NOT* say something to you like "you had no idea" or "it's not your fault." You start to think that maybe you are responsible for the result.

Here is where it gets dicey. Family members and close friends of somebody who causes either physical or mental pain in these cases ALWAYS tell the person that it's not their fault. This is true even in the cases where it was clearly the person's fault and they should have known better. I've done it myself. I might tell a close friend or family member that they shouldn't worry about the situation at all. They had nothing to do with the outcome. They should not feel responsible because they had no idea what would happen. However, what I'm really thinking is "how could you be so stupid" and "wow, this is your fault and you should own up to it." I am sure we have all experienced this first-hand.

Why do we do it? Why do we mislead close friends and family members into thinking they shouldn't feel responsible for something? I think it's easy to see that we love them, don't want them to feel bad, want to protect them and don't want them to carry around the burden of a particularly bad situation. We lie and tell half-truths in order to make sure that our loved one is okay. That's completely understandable and in most cases it's warranted. However, what effect does that have on us if that happens again and again? What it does is provide an "easy out" for somebody, meaning that they can have a situation with a negative outcome and then know that several people will tell them it's not their fault. It can turn out to be a crutch that hampers people for when they actually do need to take responsibility.

So do we stop consoling the people we care about and let them know that they shouldn't be so hard on themselves? Absolutely not. However, we need to recognize that the people who love us are being kind and are consoling us. We have to be able to be honest with ourselves and objective about situations so that we can identify if we need to take responsibility. These instances are examples of everyday occurrences that shape personal responsibility and how we view it.

3

The Self-Esteem Workshop

Self-Esteem in Education

Speaking on the telephone and consoling others are part of our informal education that we typically learn outside of school. Let's take a look at some aspects of our formal education. Our public and private education systems in the United States spend millions of dollars every year on workshops for its teachers and administrators. These workshops are aimed at keeping teachers educated on the latest trends and techniques in teaching. Keeping up-to-date on the latest ideas is good for educators. It prevents people from becoming stagnant in their knowledge and approach to their professions. Workshops and continuing education are necessary in any profession and often provide valuable information for educators. Often. Not always.

Remember the self-esteem movement in education? The reason I use the word "remember" is because it's not around anymore (if you know anybody that's still preaching this nonsense, please inform them the boat back to reality has left and they can catch it if they hurry). It's not around for good reason. While it was an interesting concept it got completely out-of-hand and took on a life of its own. There were many sincere people who believed in the power of self-esteem, but others got involved because it became a lucrative industry as well. School districts were and are willing to pay psychologists and educators to present their ideas. Further, the school districts are willing to purchase the publications and books that these professionals produce. The self-esteem movement became the foundation for many livelihoods.

Preach the word of self-esteem and get paid for it. Amazing. However, what we have found out over time is that the self-esteem movement in education was a colossal failure. It did not help children considerably. In fact, evidence exists that it may have done more harm than good.

In 1969, psychologist Nathaniel Branden published a paper called "The Psychology of Self-Esteem."[i] The basic premise of the paper is that feelings of self-esteem are the keys to success in life. The paper gained popularity and the concept grew in education circles. Throughout the 1970s and 80s a myriad of psychologists and educators conducted workshops across the country for school systems. The goal of these workshops was to inject self-esteem into the classroom. Evangelists of the movement believed that if educators could build up a student's self-esteem then that student would perform better in school and life. Endless positive reinforcement became the recipe for teachers. The movement became so popular that the California Department of Education even created a task force to promote self-esteem in 1990.[ii] Numerous school systems outlawed teachers' use of red pens for correcting papers. You see, red pen can be stressful and hurt students' feelings. That would destroy a healthy feeling of self-esteem. We wouldn't want to hurt someone's feelings by letting them know they're wrong in red pen. Tisk tisk.

"We're All Winners"

When I was in elementary school in the 1970s one of my favorite times of the year was late spring when we had "Field Day." What a great time it was. Competitive sporting events were held such as the 100-yard dash, Frisbee toss, high jump, etc. Kids would represent their individual classes and sign up for the various events to compete against each other. Of course, there was the granddaddy of the events, the Tug Of War between classes. This was the event where your class could display its physical strength as a group. After the events, the first, second and third place winners were recognized and received ribbons for their efforts. It was like a mini-Olympics and very competitive. Some kids won and others lost. What a concept. Some kids won and others lost. Did the kids who lost collapse and crumble? Were they irreparably harmed for the remainder of their childhoods and lives? Of course not. However, this type of event became scarce after the self-esteem movement took hold in education.

If you look at what many schools do today it is very much unlike what I described from my childhood. The "Field Day" event has either been eliminated or it has transformed into a carnival-like event where there are games and activities. No competitive events exist. The reason for this change is because if you have competitive events there has to be a winner or winners. If winners exist then there must be losers. The self-esteemers cannot have a situation where a child fails. That would destroy his/her self-esteem. The notions that "everyone's a winner" and "there are no failures" became prevalent in youth sports outside of the classroom as well. I cringe when in my own children's recreation athletic leagues all of the kids receive a medal for participating but no team is recognized for winning. No trophy. No recognition for doing something truly well. Nope. That would be unfair to all of the participants.

Think about what we have created by having a "no failure" environment for children where everyone is great and no one receives criticism. We have robbed a generation of children with some basic tools that will help them get through life. If somebody cannot deal with failure how on earth can they deal with life as a teenager or an adult? The fact is that you can't. As a result we have teenagers and young adults who have lived in a shielded bubble of patronizing positive reinforcement and believe that they are truly exceptional and cannot fail. It's not realistic and we have failed our children in the process.

The ramifications go well beyond that. How can we expect the United States to compete in the world if we have generations of young people who have no idea how to compete and get better as a result of failure? When you cannot deal with failure it can be very easy to slip into victim mode and blame others.

Like all "fads" or "movements" the self-esteem movement had its share of zealots that were way too enthusiastic and believed that self-esteem could possibly even cure cancer. It also had its share of promoters who pushed the concept simply for profit. Unfortunately for many taxpayers, the education system fell for the movement and its workshops hook, line and sinker. It's unfortunate because there is no evidence that this movement did any good. Thankfully, the trend in schools today seems to be to concentrate more on the basic fundamentals of education and less on the feel-good topic of self-esteem. In fact, I believe what educators are learning all over again is that nothing boosts self-esteem as well as actually achieving something. Wow! Again, what a concept.

A Little Responsibility Goes A Long Way

Here's my take on self-esteem. It's only good if you combine it with personal responsibility. This is where the movement went wrong. Believers thought that it was good enough to empower students with self-esteem. However, they left out the most important part which is using the confidence you have in yourself to be responsible for your own actions. It's very powerful. Self-esteem is the catalyst that gives you the confidence to be responsible. When you're responsible you live your life on your terms (as much as possible), you're not a victim and you have the ability to accomplish a great deal. Self-esteem by itself just creates narcissistic, unlikable, arrogant people who can't handle setbacks, failure or defeat. As a result it actually makes you weak and fragile, not strong. What makes you strong is the addition of personal responsibility.

So then what does the self-esteem movement have to do with the lack of personal responsibility in our world today? The movement was pervasive and widespread making its way out of classrooms and into the workplaces of adults. Human Resources departments embraced it and trained entire companies to implement it when evaluating employees. "Weaknesses" on evaluation forms turned into "opportunities." To insinuate that someone is "weak" in a particular area could shatter his/her self-esteem. Personally I find it amusing when my boss wants to go over my "areas of opportunity" in an evaluation. What am I, a 10-year old? Maybe if you called them "weaknesses" people would get the message and work to improve on them. This type of thinking has made everything about the individual. Many folks meander around society with highly inflated egos, brainwashed into thinking they can do no wrong. That creates much less acceptance of personal responsibility. How can something possibly be my fault when I am so great and never do anything wrong? It must be them because it's certainly not me. Scary stuff.

Should you feel good about yourself? Yes. Should you feel good about yourself because somebody tells you that you should? No. You can only fool yourself for so long. When you think about the times in your life when you felt the best about yourself I'm willing to bet they were the result of you accomplishing something. These feelings were not the result of someone patronizing you or complimenting you needlessly. Results matter and subconsciously you know that.

Let's take a look at the opposite scenario. Many people with low self-esteem tend to convert positives into negatives. For example, you may have several notable achievements in your life that you have minimized. You may have convinced yourself that a particular achievement is not that great because the task or project was not that difficult. Or you may believe that you somehow got lucky accomplishing something. This is where you need to separate the facts of your life from the emotion. You need help improving your self-esteem and the best way to do that is by building on your achievements. Write them down and look at them. Take them for what they are and not what you have turned them into with negative thinking. Again, it's the results that matter. You are personally responsible for those results and you should feel great about yourself because of them. There is no inflation of your ego without just cause. It is simply recognition of jobs well done.

By the way (or BTW as those crazy young texters type), the self-esteem movement was quickly replaced by the multi-cultural movement in education. My guess is that many of the same profiteers from the self-esteem movement went on to provide multi-cultural workshops. Thankfully that movement seems to be on the decline but that's a story for another book.

4

When In Doubt, Blame George W. Bush

Did You Ever Know That You're My Hero?

We Americans tend to go a bit overboard with popular ideas or trends of a particular era. Think about green or pink-tiled bathrooms from the 1950s and 60s. We also overdo it when we describe somebody or something with certain superlatives. For example, much tribute was given to police officers and firefighters throughout the country after the September 11th attacks. Rightfully so I might add. The word "hero" was continually used when describing the work of these public servants. I don't have an issue with throwing the word "hero" around every now and again when we talk about people who routinely put their lives on the line in their occupations. However, think about the word "hero." It is a very powerful word. Dictionary.com defines it as "a man of distinguished courage or ability, admired for his brave deeds and noble qualities." Quite fitting for cops and firefighters.

However, in true American fashion the word "hero" began to be used to describe just about every public servant during the last few months of 2001 after the September 11th attacks. I began to notice this when I heard sanitation workers and postal employees referred to as "heroes" in New York City. Don't get me wrong. There's nothing inherently bad with those occupations but look at the definition of "hero" again. Is it really appropriate to label them "heroes?" Of course, as it has been said "hindsight is 20/20." We simply tend to get caught up in the moment. How often have sports commentators and writers talked about "genius" head coaches in the National Football League? They actually compare a coach whose playoff-bound team's record is 10-6 to the likes of Einstein, Mozart and Benjamin Franklin. We do it so often that we don't even notice it anymore. When we lose our perspective on what is occurring around us we tend not to see things for what they actually are. This concept applies directly to blaming others and shirking personal responsibility.

W Did It!

In the spirit of getting caught up in the moment is the mid-to-late 2000s phenomenon of blaming George W. Bush for anything and everything. Nothing says "shirking responsibility" better than blaming the 43rd president of the United States. Why not? Everyone else is doing it. The presidential blaming became a bit popular and then downright fashionable to drop the blame on "43" for anything that went wrong.

> *Miners trapped in a collapsed mine shaft: Blame Bush. He didn't do enough to bolster mine infrastructure.*
> *Pretzel company goes out of business: Blame Bush. He almost choked on a pretzel once in the White House and destroyed the sales of pretzels worldwide.*
> *Steroids run rampant in baseball: Blame Bush. He once owned the Texas Rangers and also knows Sammy Sosa.*
> *Stimulus package not working the way it was intended: Blame Bush. He created such a bad economy that nothing can help at this point.*
> *Global warming? Bush. Illiterate adults? Bush. Women dying from plastic surgery? Bush. Potholes on the roads in winter? Bush.*

And the list goes on and on. I was once waiting for a parking attendant to retrieve my car in a garage in New

York City. As I was waiting, the manager of the garage was complaining to me about the decrease in customers that were parking cars in his garage. He was an Egyptian man and he kept saying to me "You know whose fault this is? It is the Bush." He didn't say "Bush." He said "the Bush," which made the entire conversation very entertaining. He then tried to elaborate and went onto say "...he has destroyed all of the business." As I smiled (not for the reason he thought I was smiling) I thought to myself just how sad this was. This man was blaming George Bush for the lack of cars in his garage. To no surprise, that particular manager was not employed by the garage within a few months time.

While the scope of the items attributed to the fault of George W. Bush seems humorous over time it is also quite troubling. I'm not blind to the fact that blaming a political figure occurs primarily so that an opposing political figure or group can benefit. To a great extent, that is certainly no different here. My concern is the effect that it has when it is overdone.

Many politicians have come to rely on blaming others to conceal the fact that they themselves have nothing to offer in terms of a solution. The blame game gets bigger and bigger with the net result of zero accomplishments.

People can look at it two ways. The first, and not ideal, way is to fall into the trap of copying politicians and employing blame tactics in personal and professional lives. The thought here is "...if it's good enough for them then I can do it too." The second, and preferred, way is to realize that nothing is accomplished when politicians point fingers at each other. Why on earth would you want to copy a model that has so clearly failed over time? Has it gotten people elected? Yes it has. But be smart enough to ask "What problem has it solved?" I think you will see that when you measure it in terms of societal successes versus political gain you will realize that this is not a method by which to conduct your life.

It's been my observation that people who follow politics regularly and love to talk about it frequently also feel the need to have somebody to blame for every situation. Every possible political scenario has to have someone who is a victim as well as someone to blame. The next time you're involved in a political discussion count how many times the other person says "Well, you know whose fault that is…" or "Smith was horrible. That whole crisis was his fault…" or "What is Johnson doing for those poor people. They need help…" Victims and people to blame. They're at the top of the nightly news every single day for everyone to see. In order to sell newspapers and increase viewership, news outlets need to create a good story. What better way to do that then create the age-old story of the good guy versus the bad guy? It's just like a television show. Wait, the nightly news is a television show. Do you think there could be a connection to people thinking that they are victims and blaming others in their personal lives? It makes sense that if you hear it every day then it would have some effect on you.

Politics as Sport

It could also be that we have become accustomed to blaming whoever is in charge. Sports are like politics in several ways. They are both very popular with many people following the latest happenings. They are also both very popular topics of discussion in the news, the office, the home and at social gatherings. Inevitably the conversation turns to a team that is not performing well. People may blame the head coach or manager of the team for the poor performance. Now let's be realistic. The coach may get the blame just about all of the time but it's not always his or her fault. It's not even close. The coach can't hit a baseball, make a tackle or shoot a basketball. At some point teams have to execute in order to be successful. But coaches are judged by results and not necessarily whether they put together a good game plan or prepared the players well. That's just the way it is in professional and big-time college sports. The average tenure of a head coach in the National Football League is about 2.5 years.[iii] That's an average. So it's obvious that coaches are on a short leash with management and the fans.

We know that sports and politics are two of the most popular topics for us to discuss AND they are covered every day in news broadcasts. We also know that a good portion of what we read and hear as it relates to those topics is people getting blamed for things that have gone wrong. After a while it becomes second nature for us to read the reports and listen to the broadcasts that include the finger-pointing. It's almost expected. I believe that we are seriously affected by the mass-media blitz of blaming. How could we not be? Or maybe it's just "the Bush's" fault.

5

The Nanny State Enablers

Cradle to Grave Blaming

Don't you just love it when somebody makes a decision on your behalf and then forces you to comply with it? If you're like most people then you don't appreciate it one bit. Yet we continue to allow our governments to decide what is good for us. Why? The answer is because we have been lulled into a sense of false security that our government is going to take care of us in every aspect of our lives.

Today when I walk into a fast food restaurant in New York City I am informed of the calorie content for the meal I am about to order. Some would argue that calorie information is helpful and gives people necessary information to make good choices. Displaying calorie information by itself is what I would consider passive. However there is a downside to this type of governing that contributes to "the blame game."

What happens if a restaurant does not display that information on a menu? And what if I become hideously obese as a result? What if my obesity leads to depression and a physical and mental inability to hold employment? I hope you see where this is going and why lawyers are the ones that create laws. Aside from the fact that attorneys guarantee themselves employment through lawsuits, think about the blaming potential with these laws. Whether you agree with these type of "nanny state" laws and regulations is not the issue. The point is that our own government is significantly contributing to our lack of personal responsibility. Years from now people will be saying "How can anyone expect me to eat this when there is no calorie posting for it? What is this, the dark ages?" Isn't it interesting that fast food restaurants existed in the United States from the 1950s through the 1980s without the obesity epidemic that we have today? Why? We know it's not because calorie content was posted in the restaurants. It has a lot to do with people making better choices with regard to diet and physical activity.

Just think how lucky you are if you live in San Francisco. The city government is so concerned with your well being that it banned the sale of most Happy Meals offered by McDonald's.[iv] The ordinance bans restaurants from offering a free toy with a meal if that meal does not meet set levels of calorie, sugar and fat content...as determined by the city government. The ordinance forces fast food restaurants to offer alternatives such as fruit and milk with the meal. So much for the free market. I mean it's not like California has bigger problems to tackle such as a gigantic fiscal crisis that most countries could never even dream of accumulating. However I digress.

That brings us to accepting the situation. The fast food examples are microcosms of a litany of government regulations designed to make us do what is right (as deemed by the government). Everything from what light bulbs we have to use to how much trash we can generate. What if we were to turn every one of these situations around and look at them differently? What if they were actually empowering and not restricting?

I am personally responsible for what I eat and how much I exercise. I don't need to be dependent on the government to tell me what I should or shouldn't be eating. If I become unhealthy as a result of my diet it is my fault and nobody else's. Free toy or not.

I am personally responsible for my electricity bill and the amount of electricity my house generates. I know there are energy saving alternatives available and I can install them. I don't need to be dependent on the government to tell me that I have to change my bulbs. If my bill is out of control and I have to change light bulbs every year then it is my fault and nobody else's.

I am personally responsible for the amount of things I throw away on a weekly basis. I know there are multiple ways to recycle and reuse items. I don't need the government to tell me how much trash I can generate. If we need more landfills then it is partially my fault.

The list can go on to include so many things in your life. What is truly powerful about those statements of personal responsibility is that they are liberating. You are freeing yourself from the shackles of another entity dictating what you can or cannot do. It is totally up to you. Once you accept and own it then you can deal with it. Instead of wandering around and being told what to do, you actually take the reins of life and gain some control.

It's All Gone to the Dogs

Did you know that the City of San Francisco has a housing code – for doghouses?[v] Yes, doghouses. I'm not making this up. I'm not trying to pick on San Francisco. I've been there several times and have always enjoyed it. However the politicians are particularly prolific at producing ridiculous laws. They have made it very easy to cite examples of nanny state laws.

A housing code for dogs. It makes me laugh every time I think about it. Many third-world countries don't have any housing codes for their citizens yet we are so advanced that we have a city in which there is a housing code for its dogs. I have to imagine that word has gotten out in the doggy community and many canines have picked up and moved to the City by the Bay. The way I understand it is that you can sell an attractive 3-bedroom doghouse in most parts of the country and barely have enough money to buy a 1-bedroom fixer-upper doghouse in San Francisco. Dog real estate is through the roof there.

Do I necessarily need the government to tell me exactly how to build a house for my dog? I'm sure the code was created with the best of intentions, as is the case with most nanny state ordinances. However, did we elect politicians to micro manage our lives to the point of telling us how we should house our pets? While it's not shocking that cities such as New York or San Francisco will have many of the "we know what's good for you" types of laws, it's concerning that personal freedom is being chipped away at. Man has always struggled to find the balance between chaos and order. It's like a pendulum that sways back and forth with each group or person determining what the correct balance should be. At the rate many of these nanny state laws are being passed we will need a book to refer to when we get out of bed in the morning. That book will tell us how we should proceed with our day. What's permissible and what's not. What can I cook? How should I drive? How long can I stay in the shower? How much toilet paper can I use? What type of shingles can I put on my dog's house?

What I'm getting at is the more nanny state laws we put on the books, the less we become dependent on ourselves and more dependent on government telling us what to do. In other words, we lose our independence. If you don't have independence you can't have personal responsibility. The notion that government knows best is very dangerous. The danger that I'm talking about is not in the areas that nanny state laws cover. I'm talking about the areas where it does NOT cover. It's very easy for me slip into a mode of thinking where I don't feel any responsibility for anything not covered by laws or ordinances. For example, there's no law regarding how much I can sit on the couch during the day therefore I don't need to be responsible for my lack of activity. It's the government's fault that they don't have that law. That's an extreme example but it is exactly where we are headed in our conditioning if we don't snap out of it and think for ourselves.

6

I've Fallen and Can't Get Up

I Got Screwed!

We've already seen how the lack of personal responsibility and dealing with setbacks are prevalent in our schools, media, politics and everyday lives. Now think back to a time in your own life when you got the short end of the stick. When you were taken advantage of. When you were totally right. Basically think of a time when you got screwed. I'm sure we can all think of these times. Think about Lucy taking away the football from Charlie Brown or the baseball going through Bill Buckner's legs in Game 6 of the '86 World Series.

Let me share a story about someone who was treated unfairly and could not understand why. Names are changed to protect the innocent. Jim was a hard working and trustworthy teenager. During the summer he worked part-time at a small marine/scuba company that a local family owned. He showed a real knack for the job and the environment and demonstrated continuously that this was not simply a job for him. Beyond being a skilled worker, he offered suggestions on how to make the business better. He always worked extra hours or at times when he was asked to fill in for others. Jim even took special classes to become certified to teach scuba diving and windsurfing. As time went on he became very friendly with the family that owned the company. Eventually he was considered part of the family. Jim had his own key to the shop and was trusted with some financial operations as well.

Jim moved on to college but came back during breaks to work at the company. He was always welcomed back and looked forward to returning. The job allowed him to mature in a business environment and helped to prepare him for his future. His relationship with the family that owned the company could not have been better. In fact, he really felt like he was an extended family member.

At the end of his junior year in college, Jim began to contemplate exactly what he wanted to do after school. An internship for the summer break period opened up for a company that Jim was very interested in working at. He applied for the internship and landed the position. Once he had cemented his plans he informed the family that owned the marine/scuba business that he was not going to return for the summer. It was very difficult for him but he knew that he had to plan for his future. The family understood and wished him well.

During the first semester of Jim's senior year he began to plan for the Christmas break period. He assumed that the family he had befriended would welcome him back for the break and allow him to work there. However when he had contacted the family about it they told him that they did not want him to work there anymore. Furthermore they had remembered that he had a key to the shop and they needed it back.

Needless to say, Jim was very hurt. He would talk about how he couldn't believe that he spent so much time at and worked so hard for that company and they threw him out instantly. He felt used and of course grew apart from the family. How could they do this to him? How could they reject someone who gave so much to them? This was not fair to say the least. He had been the model employee and this is how he was treated. Unbelievable.

Or Did I?

It's important for us to be able to view these types of situations in our lives from all perspectives. When we only see from our own viewpoint we don't get the whole picture. There is information in this story that I left out and is very useful to know when thinking about who is wrong or right. When Jim was thinking about his future during college he never once talked about it with the family that owned the business. He never told them what he was thinking. He never consulted them or asked for advice. He never asked if they had plans for him after his college days.

Years later Jim ran into the father of the family at a restaurant. Each one inquired about how the other was doing. The conversation eventually turned to the past and how Jim felt slighted that he was not welcomed back to the company to work. The father explained to Jim just how hurt the entire family was when Jim had informed them of his decision to take the internship and pursue other interests between his junior and senior years. The family felt that they had developed a bond with the young man and believed that he was going to be a significant part of the future business. Jim's news of leaving them was dropped on them like a bombshell and they felt betrayed. They had no idea he was thinking of working somewhere else. They thought that they were developing the perfect young employee who had a bright future with them. It was hard for the family to take and made them tentative about becoming close with any employee after that. When Jim inquired about coming back during Christmas break the family could not open that door again.

Jim soon realized that he was not innocent in this case. He had always looked at it from his own viewpoint. When things did not go his way he became a victim. He would tell friends and relatives about how the family was thankless and hurt him tremendously. Jim was wearing the figurative glasses that all victims wear. They only see things from their own perspective. Once he took those glasses off and was able to see from the other side it became clear to him that he was not the victim. The feelings that he felt right before Christmas break were the very same feelings that the family felt when Jim decided to go elsewhere with his internship. Taking off those glasses was enlightening and allowed him to see clearly.

Think for yourself about those times I asked you to recall at the beginning of the chapter. Remember all of the instances where you told others about them and how you were the victim. Now think about all of the other possible perspectives involved in those situations. Is it possible that maybe, just maybe, you weren't the victim that you thought you were all this time? Is it possible that maybe you contributed to the outcome? Were there obvious signs that you ignored? Did others warn you about the potential negative outcome? My guess is that the answer is yes to any one of those questions.

Believe it or not, being a victim is something that many people enjoy. We have all experienced friends or relatives who love to tell stories about how they got screwed. No matter what the situation is, that person is getting the short end of the stick. It actually becomes an identity for some and is difficult to shed. Being a victim is easy. It's the lazy person's way out. Is it easier to lie on the couch and watch TV or get up and exercise for 45 minutes? For most people the couch option is way easier. It's the same thing with victimhood. Blaming others is always the easy way out. What we need to do is get up off the couch and start looking at things from other viewpoints...objectively.

Just like exercising, it becomes easier to do once we start and practice it for a while. Before you know it, you become stronger every day as a result.

7

"But he started it!"

Are You Acting Like My Kids?

If you are or have ever been a parent, sibling or child the following will sound very familiar to you. My wife and I have had a conversation with our two boys that goes something like this (and oh by the way we've had this conversation a few hundred times):

10-year old: (Shouting at 8-year old) "Stop it! Stop it!"

8-year old: (Laughing) "No. You leave me alone."

10-year old: "I said to stop it!"

8-year old: "Give me back the remote!"

10-year old: "Get out of here!"

At this point some type of physical interaction begins to occur. It typically involves wrestling and pushing. Depending on where we are on the patience-level meter one of us will interject.

Parent: "Guys, knock it off."

Both boys in stereo: "He started it."

Both boys in stereo to each other: "No you started it!"

Parent: "It doesn't matter. What's going on here?"

8-year old: "He took the remote and now we're watching his show."

10-year old: "Go somewhere else and watch your show."

8-year old: "You go somewhere else."

Parent: "Whoa, whoa. Hold on guys. Listen. Let's put something on that you can both agree on."

Now once the immediate issue is settled, in this case it's a battle for the television remote control, I'll speak with them about how they need to act in the future and how they shouldn't fight with each other over such miniscule issues.

For this situation I address both of them by talking about how ridiculous it is to argue over a television show. I then move onto how there is more than one television in the house and they don't necessarily have to watch the same show. At this point I move into the real meat of the issue. First, there is the topic of not taking something from somebody (the remote). Second, there is the issue of resorting to violence over a disagreement. Third, I give a superbly wonderful speech about how not everybody wants to do the same thing all of the time. If they want to make it in life they have to compromise. Going off to college and living with other people forces you to compromise. Having a relationship with a girlfriend or wife forces you to compromise. Your work life will be filled with compromises. If you don't learn how to get along then you will have a very difficult life. I then list some examples of compromises I make in my everyday life.

Now that order is restored, I'm thoroughly impressed with myself and my parenting skills. I then wrap up the conversation by asking them if they understand and that we're clear on the situation. Inevitably the answer I get is this:

10-year old: "Yeah but he started it."

8-year old: "No you started it!"

While it's humorous to recount these stories they are beyond frustrating at the time. The reason I bring it up is because neither one of the boys is open to changing at that time. They see the situation at hand, which is all that they're concerned about. No attention is paid whatsoever to the big picture or how to correct the situation. The prevailing attitude is "I'm right. I want to watch my show. He started it. End of story." I could talk to them for hours about the virtues of getting along and compromising and it would make no difference at that moment. As a parent I just hope that over time some of my incredible parental wisdom makes it through to their brains and they become better people as a result. The question for you is "Are you ready?" Will you have a closed mind like my 8 and 10-year old boys fighting with each other? Or will you embrace the advice and change? Let's face it. Have we been acting like children?

Open Up and Let the Sunshine In

Did it really matter who started the argument between my boys? If you answered "yes" then you are not ready to accept personal responsibility and change. If you answered "no, of course not" then you are in the right frame of mind to get your life on track. This is the most important step in making any significant change. We've all heard or experienced first-hand how addicts cannot change their behavior until they admit their addiction and realize that they want and need to change. We've also all heard the expression, misattributed to several authors and scientists, "The definition of insanity is doing something the same way over and over again and expecting a different result."

Isn't it interesting how both of my boys sounded like helpless victims in their interaction with me? "But he started it." The reason is because they have yet to open their minds to taking the initiative to change the situation. If I don't interject who knows how long they'll go on saying the same things back and forth and eventually fighting. It's that closed-mindedness that is causing them to act like victims. Once they realize that they can each take more productive actions to fix the situation they have become personally accountable. Mind you that I'm talking about an 8 and 10-year old. I expect them to fight like that as is the case with just about every other boy who ever lived. I expect them to blame each other and anything else they can think of to avoid getting into trouble with Dad. But what is your excuse? What are you waiting for?

You have two choices. The first one is to act like a child, cross your arms, shake your head and say "No thanks." The second one is to have an open mind. A mind that can take in new ideas and explore different ways of accomplishing things. A mind that understands that it needs to change in order to gain control and solve problems. A mind that is tired of acting like a doormat and leaving its life up to others. To me the choice is clear and I hope it is for you as well. Think of all of the things you want to change in your life and ask yourself "If not me then who?" Once you realize the answer to that question is "nobody" then you need to take the next step and rise up from victimhood.

8

Jump In. The Water's Fine.

The Changing of the Guard

Like any other significant change that you make in your life you have to be ready. The previous chapter discussed getting into the right frame of mind. Once you are ready it's time to put the blaming days behind you and move in a direction defined by positivity. But how?

Start with something simple and build on it. It's a concept that is tried and true for good reason. Think about any major product that is launched into the marketplace. Before the launch occurs the product is tested and then possibly introduced to a small geographic market or perhaps several companies or individuals for beta-testing. If the tests and pre-release feedback are positive then the company moves ahead with launching the product. It's a very logical approach. Think about that when making an attitude change in your life such as this. Pick an item or two where you can test out the theory and see it in action.

I'll use an example from my own life. I have a dog that happens to be very handsome like his owner. He's a good size at 65 pounds and is extremely lovable. One major problem exists with him. He pees like a girl. That's right. He pees like a girl. I'm insulting my dog with the age-old insult used to insult someone's manhood. The truth is that he refuses to lift his leg on a fence or a tree or anything else that stands upright. He squats on various parts of my lawn and urinates the way that a female dog would. That in and of itself is not an issue. However the result is that after a couple of days, the grass burns out in the spot where he relieved himself. Over the course of a week there are several noticeable brown spots that develop and destroy the beauty of my lawn.

This situation is extremely frustrating because I work very hard on my lawn to make it look good. The appeal of the lawn adds to the overall attractiveness of the house. It is very discouraging for me to put in all of the effort of planting seed, watering, cutting, trimming and fertilizing only to have it obliterated by a dog that refuses to lift his leg and act like a man! For a while I shrugged it off and said "oh well, that's what I get for having a dog." I would then complain about it and tell people that I can't have a nice looking lawn because my dog ruins it. The situation was hopeless.

Then I decided to do something different. I changed my weekly routine of cutting the grass to incorporate something additional. I figured out that the way to rid my lush green lawn of these spots was to pull up the dead, brown grass, dig and mix up the dirt, plant new seed and water the spots. Within about 7-10 days new grass comes in. Every week when I finish cutting the lawn I dig up and replant about 5 or 6 spots. It has worked out quite well and the lawn looks beautiful as long as I remain consistent with the new routine. There are never more than a couple to a few spots that need repair. A little bit of extra time spent every week has made a world of difference.

I went from blaming a dog for a poor lawn to taking control and vastly improving my situation. At some point I had had enough with the status quo, took responsibility and actually accomplished something. Now let's be real here. A lawn is nothing compared to the significant issues that you have in your life. But that is my point. Start with something that is small in the grand scheme of your existence. It's the process that matters. Once it is successful build on it. The same frame of mind exists for the things that really matter.

It has been empowering for me to realize that my lawn looks beautiful because I took control of it. My self-confidence has risen considerably as it relates to home improvement and I've been able to take on more jobs at home as a result. And it's all because I took responsibility. The combination of responsibility, self-esteem and achievement has created a positive snowball effect and given me the ability look differently at all of the home improvement issues waiting to be addressed.

> *The kids aren't to blame for the broken doorknob. I'm in charge of the house and I can replace it.*

> *The contractor isn't to blame for the drafty door. I can easily adjust it and install weather stripping.*

> *Bugs aren't to blame for almost killing one of my plants. I can talk to a garden expert at a local nursery and take the steps necessary to eliminate the bugs.*

It is amazing to see the transformation from weakness to strength in a short period of time. Can this translate into other parts of your life? Absolutely. The process is the same. Instead of home improvement it could be a bad situation at work. Forget about placing blame as to why the situation is bad. Just accept the facts and use them to your advantage. Take some time to write down various ways that you could take some control of the situation to make it better. For example, it's possible that you're not advancing in your company or you feel underappreciated at work. You've been blaming your boss because she has her favorite employees and you're not one of them. You need to do a few things that could help.

First, be honest about evaluating the situation. Think about the chapter where we talked about each person involved in the situation having different perspectives. Consider your boss' viewpoint. Try to put yourself in her position and be as objective as possible. Once you've done that you may realize that she's not playing favorites and she has some legitimate reasons for promoting others or issuing better assignments to other employees.

Second, come up with various ways that you could be seen in a better light. You could create a list of several items that could help you to boost your internal image, become better ingratiated with your boss and show that you're willing and capable of taking on new projects. Are you seen as a negative or positive force in the office? If it's negative then you need to fix that so as not to bring everyone down.

Third, you can ask for an expectations review meeting with your boss. Maybe the two of you are simply not connecting because her expectations are different than yours. The main point is that you are analyzing the situation and thinking about ways that you can make it better. There is no wringing of hands or dwelling on the past that cannot be changed. You are beginning to take an active role in making a better future.

At the conclusion of the exercise you may have half a dozen items written down that you can act on. You've completed a major step in the process by having a plan. Now you have to execute and put the plan into action.

I Want a New Drug

Once a successful outcome is realized and replicated, the empowerment is like a drug. You begin to look for things to change that need improvement. A new outlook takes over. What used to be a hopeless mess turns into a problem that you can fix. It becomes something positive in your life. Today it's the spots on the lawn. Tomorrow it's my weight. Next week it's a broken relationship. I can do it all.

That brings us to the opposite problem. Just as with any drug, you have to control it. I'll stick with the home improvement theme and tell you about the time I received a new power washer as a gift. I knew that I had a couple of items that needed to be cleaned with the power washer. I opened it up and tested it out. Everything worked great. After fiddling around with some of the attachments I got to work. I used it on my patio and deck. It was unbelievable how much dirt came off. Everything looked brand new when I was done. Well the results were intoxicating. I had the power washer gun in my hand and was looking for anything that needed to be cleaned. The fence looked dirty. So did the basketball backboard. Some toys were looking shabby. What about the mailbox? The foundation of the house could use a good scrub. Now that I think of it the dog looks like he needs to be washed. The kids too. This thing is great! I am cleaning everything in my path. Get out of my way!

Obviously if I had tackled everything that came into my mind the results would not have been good. Something would not have turned out the way I was hoping. Worse yet, something would have broken or somebody would have gotten hurt. So it's important to take things slow and think them through. Starting small and building is the best way to gain the confidence necessary to take on responsibility in your life. After all, it's a major life change – a whole new way of thinking. The biggest mistake you can make is trying to take on everything at one time.

9
No One is to Blame

Sweet Serenity

It's important for you to notice that in the examples regarding the home improvement projects and workplace issues I listed in the previous chapter I did not blame anyone or anything. More importantly I did not blame myself when speaking about my personal situation. It's very easy to take my advice and simply place the blame you've been directing elsewhere and dump it onto yourself. That is worse than your current situation. When I talk about freeing yourself from "the blame game" that includes self blame.

Blame is not important and offers no solution. Accepting responsibility and acting to remedy a situation is the equivalent of saying "I got this." We need to move on from blaming and start acting. Let's not wait for others to fix things. Let's be part of the solution and stop dwelling on the problem. That's what personal responsibility is all about. Take a look at the very famous Serenity Prayer attributed to theologian Reinhold Niebuhr[vi]:

> *God, grant me the serenity to accept the things I cannot change, Courage to change the things I can, And wisdom to know the difference.*

The prayer is so powerful and wise that it is used by several twelve-step addiction programs including Alcoholics Anonymous. When I look at this prayer I feel a sense of self-empowerment. It is about acceptance and realizing that there are things that can be changed in life.

It's interesting to note that nowhere in the prayer does it say "grant me the wisdom to blame others or myself." And with good reason. Acceptance is a huge part of personal responsibility. We need to accept situations and skip over the part where we used to blame others. The Serenity Prayer helps us to move forward. Blaming does the opposite. It anchors us into the bad situation of the past. We need to accept, change what we can and make the best of what we can't.

Whenever we are "anchored" to something we are prisoners. But we don't have to be. We are prisoners by our own choices. Claiming our independence from "the blame game" starts with the realization that there is no prison guard. Nobody is standing outside your cell with a set of keys preventing you from escaping. You are the guard. You have the keys. You can walk right out of the cell, collect your belongings and drive away from the prison. Once you start pointing the finger of blame at others or yourself it's like throwing yourself back into the prison.

Let the World Go By

Part of the accepting process is knowing that the world around you is not going to change. You will continue to receive lame excuses from people not getting back to you. You'll also continue to see politicians on television blaming somebody for poor results. Government will continue to pry into your personal life more and more and try to take responsibility away from you. And the list will go on and on. You have to see all of those distractions for what they are, namely distractions. Now you'll be able to do that because you can quickly recognize them. All of the societal factors that contribute to "the blame game" are typically not recognized and exist without too much fanfare or notice. However, based on what you have read here you'll be able to notice them immediately. In fact, you'll start noticing them again and again to the point where you'll wonder why you hadn't seen them all along.

It's comparable to when you make a major purchase such as an automobile or a large appliance. Say you recently bought a black Ford Edge®. You never really noticed them on the road before. But now that you've bought the vehicle, it seems like you're seeing them everywhere. You wonder how you never noticed all of the black Ford Edge automobiles that are on the road.

The best advice is to recognize the needless blaming and chuckle. Use it as motivation. Adopt the mindset that you are stronger than "the blame game" nonsense that goes on around you and sucks so many people into the vortex of inadequacy and failure. You're better than that and it's amusing to see so many others wasting their time. Think of it as remaining above the fray.

It's perfectly fine for you to come to the understanding that it's all about you. Yes, it is. We've heard people tell each other "it's not all about you" when they're calling out that someone is being selfish and self-centered. However when it comes to taking control of your own life it *IS* all about you. No one else is going to take control of it for you. Remember that as you remain above the fray. You will not allow the idiocy beneath you to drag you down. Victims allow themselves to get dragged down and you're not one of them.

A good example of this is found in a typical workplace. Just about everyone has experienced one or two people who are negative about everything. It doesn't matter whether it is a major initiative the company is undertaking or simply purchasing a new coffee machine. These people will find the most negative things to say about the company. If you speak with them at lunch or around the proverbial water cooler you inevitably get lulled into their negative-speak. Suddenly you start to believe them and you become irritated and agitated. These people are like a cancer in an organization. The negative venom spreads and paralyzes departments and entire organizations.

The recommended course of action is to steer clear of the "Negative Nellies" and "Debbie Downers" in the office. It can be difficult but remember it is about you and your mindset. When encountered by these folks just keep in mind one thing. Think about any of the top personnel at any company you have ever known. Were they negative people? Now think about any of the negative people you've encountered at companies where you have worked. What positions did they hold? I know that you'll find there is a relationship there. Successful people are not negative. The last thing you should do is take the negative road and assume that successful people received good breaks and that's why they're in charge of the company. That is not reality at all. The overwhelming majority of successful people have worked hard and earned their positions. The bottom line is that you don't want to be a part of that as no good comes from it.

Similar outcomes will occur with "the blame game." Be careful not to get drawn back into that mindset. Just like the "Negative Nellies", it's a no-win situation.

You'll also notice that many of these people are conspiracy theorists. Give it a try in the office. After a negative rant, ask them if they believe the CIA killed President Kennedy or if the U.S. government knew about 9/11 before it happened.

10

Freedom Calls. Will You Answer?

Nothing to Lose

The ball is in your court now. Will you continue to be dependent upon the actions of others? Is being a victim the best way to live your life? Will blaming others improve your situation? Are people going to congregate around you and hold a pity party in your honor? The answer to all of those questions is "no." Not just "no" but a resounding and emphatic "no."

I started this book in the first chapter with the joke about the priest in the flooded church. God sent him two boats and a helicopter and he made the wrong choice every time. It's a funny story as long as it remains a story. It becomes sad when you're talking about your own life. The opportunities are there and they present themselves every single day. No one will send you an invitation and ask you to change your life. You have got to make that decision for yourself and start right now. Not next week or when it's more convenient. Right now.

I sometimes hear people say about a negative person "Oh he just likes to play the victim." Who wants to play the victim, let alone enjoy doing it? It would be like playing a game and enjoying losing all of the time. Somebody might ask you to play a game and you say "Great. Let's play. I can't wait to lose." Does anybody actually adopt that mindset? No sane person gets involved in a game with the objective of losing. Why would we then do that in life?

I understand that people don't act on certain things in their lives because of the fear of failure. Many internal reasons exist that cause that. What I'm asking is to view your negative situations a bit differently. Don't think about failing. Look at the situation as not being able to get worse. Don't think of yourself as the person that we're all counting on to make things work. That scenario is filled with high-pressure that can turn many people off. Think of yourself as the person that's been called in to clean things up. It's not going to be easy but you're going to get a lot of leeway in the process. You have nothing to lose. And that's exactly how you have to look at it – you have nothing to lose.

Rehabilitate Your Outlook

When people undergo surgery to repair a joint or limb they typically attend physical rehabilitation sessions after the surgery is performed. The rehabilitation is the best way for them to regain the strength that they once had in a knee or an ankle. It also retrains them to walk, jump and run. Physical rehabilitation is not too far removed from escaping victimhood. You need to undergo a process that retrains the way that you think and makes you stronger.

The optimal way to rehabilitate your outlook is to put your new attitude into practice. I've given you a couple of ideas to get started with the key underlying premise that starting small and working your way up is the best method. Once you're up and running you've got to keep going until it becomes routine. Again, it's just like physical rehabilitation. Practice and practice until it becomes routine.

The biggest difference between your former outlook and your new outlook is that you are actually conscious about having an outlook and mindset. You are thinking about how you think. Sounds strange but it's true. Previously you probably never realized that there was a pattern to your thinking and it was somehow connected to all of the situations in your life. Now that you know that, you can use it to your advantage.

There's a concept in sports called "muscle memory." Basically it is training your muscles to perform certain movements without you having to think about them. For example, when a young player is being taught how to properly swing a baseball bat, a good hitting coach will show him the various stages of the swing and how they should be swinging the bat. These include actions that at first seem awkward such as twisting the hips and back foot in the midst of the swing. We are not programmed to perform those movements in our everyday lives. When children first practice those movements you can see them thinking about them. Sometimes they swing using the proper technique and sometimes they don't. The coach is counting on "muscle memory" to kick in over time. If the swing is repeated properly over and over again it will become engrained into the player's memory and he will not have to think about it anymore. Eventually the player will swing naturally and utilize the proper movement every time. This is also why bad swings are difficult to correct. The brain and muscles need to be retrained.

I believe that this concept holds true for how we think. It is also the main reason why I suggest starting small and working your way up. We need to practice in order to get it right. And we need to seriously think about the process. It is going to take some time to change the way that we've been thinking for years. Being the victim has been convenient. It's allowed you to have an excuse for every scenario. It's enabled you choose the path of least resistance. Of course, as you know by now, it has also created many undesirable outcomes in your life. It will take time and practice.

Great news is here though. You can start immediately. The basic tools already exist – you and your brain. Plenty of opportunities are present as well. The big question is "Will you make the change?" As I said before, you have nothing to lose. Assuming more personal responsibility in your life is extremely powerful. It is the crucial component enabling you to break free.

Remember these tips to get you through:

If you're debating whether you're ready to change your attitude, ask yourself "If not me then who?"

Blaming doesn't exist anymore. Do not blame other people, entities, situations and certainly not yourself.

Pick one area in your life, perhaps a minor area where you want to make a change and improve the condition.

Accept the situation for what it is.

Be as objective as possible and try to see from other points of view.

Get creative and make a list of possible solutions that you can implement.

Execute and make a conscious effort to think about the way you think. And then execute again and again.

Evaluate your results and move onto other areas of your life. Rinse. Repeat. And rinse again.

Remember to start slowly and don't take on too much at one time.

Nobody ever sets out to be a victim. It happens unknowingly and slowly over time. It's time for you to take control and achieve on your own terms. You don't need a permission slip to become empowered. It's up to you. Don't let the opportunity pass you by. Answer the call and break free from "the blame game." You'll see how quickly you go from being a victim to victory.

About the Author

Joe McGuire has worked in the high-tech business field for 20 years. His office experiences have given him a front row seat to just about every responsibility shirking antic available. Whether it is an executive want-to-be jockeying for position or someone simply being lazy, the corporate world has provided endless fodder for "the blame game."

Joe has always enjoyed writing and putting his talents to use for commercial purposes such as product description sheets, ad copy and general marketing materials. Combining a sense of humor, an ability to not take himself so seriously, a knack for writing and societal observations seemed like a natural fit.

Joe lives in New Jersey with his wife, Sue, and two children. You can visit his website at www.josephemcguire.com.

Works Cited

[i] http://en.wikipedia.org/wiki/Nathaniel_Branden

[ii] http://www.eric.ed.gov/ERICWebPortal/search/detailmini.jsp?_nfpb=true&_&ERICExtSearch_SearchValue_0=ED321170&ERICExtSearch_SearchType_0=no&accno=ED321170

[iii] http://www.sportsbusinessdaily.com/Journal/Issues/2009/02/20090209/Opinion/NFL-Head-Coaches-Hold-The-Toughest-CEO-Job-In-America.aspx

[iv] http://articles.latimes.com/2010/nov/02/business/la-fi-happy-meals-20101103

[v] http://articles.sfgate.com/2005-01-07/bay-area/17358106_1_doghouses-housing-code-new-law

[vi] http://en.wikipedia.org/wiki/Serenity_Prayer

www.ingramcontent.com/pod-product-compliance
Lightning Source LLC
Chambersburg PA
CBHW051244170526
45165CB00004B/1574